# PREDATOR VS PREY

# Crocodile Vs Wildebeest

Mary Meinking

Raintree

**www.raintreepublishers.co.uk**
Visit our website to find out
more information about
Raintree books.

**To order:**
☎ Phone 0845 6044371
📄 Fax +44 (0) 1865 312263
⌨ Email myorders@raintreepublishers.co.uk

Customers from outside the UK please telephone +44 1865 312262

Raintree is an imprint of Capstone Global Library Limited,
a company incorporated in England and Wales having its
registered office at 7 Pilgrim Street, London, EC4V 6LB –
Registered company number: 6695582

Text © Capstone Global Library Limited 2011
First published in hardback in 2011
The moral rights of the proprietor have
been asserted.

Edited by Rebecca Rissman, Dan Nunn,
    and Catherine Veitch
Designed by Joanna Hinton Malivoire
Levelling by Jeanne Clidas
Picture research by Hannah Taylor
Production by Victoria Fitzgerald
Originated by Capstone Global Library
Printed and bound in China by CTPS

ISBN 978 1 406 21865 7
14 13 12 11 10
10 9 8 7 6 5 4 3 2 1

**British Library Cataloguing in Publication Data**
Meinking, Mary.
Crocodile vs wildebeest. -- (Predator vs prey)
591.5'3-dc22
A full catalogue record for this book is available from the
British Library.

**Acknowledgements**
We would like to thank the following for permission
to reproduce photographs: ardea.com pp. 27 (© Ferrero-
Labat), 28 (© Ferrero- Labat); Corbis pp. 23 (Andy Rouse),
25 (Joe McDonald); FLPA pp. 4 (Ariadne Van Zandbergen), 8
(Malcolm Schuyl), 13 (Ariadne Van Zandbergen), 17 (Minden
Pictures/ Suzi Eszterhas), 19 (Minden Pictures/ Suzi Eszterhas),
21 (Minden Pictures/ Suzi Eszterhas), 18 (Minden Pictures/
Suzi Eszterhas); Getty Images p. 10 (Gallo Images/ Federico
Veronesi); istockphoto p. 6 (©Catharina van den Dikkenberg);
NHPA p. 29 (Martin Harvey); Photolibrary pp. 5 (Peter
Arnold Images/ Martin Harvey), 9 (Imagestate/ Jonathan
& Angela Scott), 12 (Oxford Scientific/ Roger de la Harpe),
14 (age fotostock/ Anup Shah), 15 (age fotostock/ Thomas
Dressler), 16 (John Warburton-Lee Photography/ Nigel Pavitt),
20 (Oxford Scientific/ Mark Deeble & Victoria Stone), 24
(John Warburton-Lee Photography/Nigel Pavitt), 26 (Oxford
Scientific/ Mike Powles); Rex Features p. 22 (Andy Rouse);
shutterstock pp. 7 (©EcoPrint), 11 (©EcoPrint).

Cover photographs of a Nile crocodile reproduced with
permission of FLPA (Malcolm Schuyl), and a wildebeest
reproduced with permission of shutterstock (© EcoPrint).

We would like to thank Michael Bright for his invaluable help
in the preparation of this book.

Every effort has been made to contact copyright holders of
material reproduced in this book. Any omissions will
be rectified in subsequent printings if notice is given to the
publisher.

**Disclaimer**
All the Internet addresses (URLs) given in this book were valid
at the time of going to press. However, due to the dynamic
nature of the Internet, some addresses may have changed, or
sites may have changed or ceased to exist since publication.
While the author and publisher regret any inconvenience this
may cause readers, no responsibility for any such changes can
be accepted by either the author or the publisher.

Some words are shown in bold, **like this**. You can find
out what they mean by looking in the glossary.

# Contents

# Teeth vs horns

Jaws crush! Hooves stomp! Two animals battle on the riverbank. On one side of the battle is the crocodile. Its teeth are sharp and it is ready for action!

crocodile

The other animal in the fight is the wildebeest. Both animals are ready for a fight!

wildebeest

The competitors live in Africa. Both have strengths that will help them in this battle.

## PREDATOR
### Nile crocodile

LENGTH: 6 metres

WEIGHT: 680 kilograms

STRENGTH: swallows rocks to help it stay underwater

**Key**

 where Nile crocodiles and blue wildebeest live

# PREY
## blue wildebeest

**LENGTH:** 2.4 metres

**WEIGHT:** 230 kilograms

**STRENGTH:** runs very fast on land

Africa

# Toothy grin

The crocodile is a killing machine! Its eyes, ears, and **nostrils** are on the top of its head. This is handy when it is underwater sneaking up on **prey**.

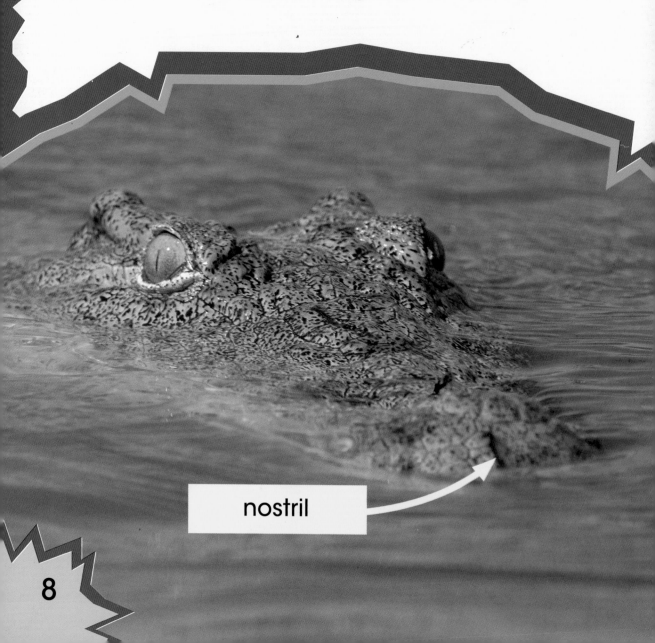

nostril

**DID YOU KNOW?**
Crocodiles can snap their jaws shut harder than any other animal on Earth!

# Thundering hooves

The wildebeest's feet, or **hooves**, are its best protection. If a predator attacks a young wildebeest, the **herd** surrounds the predator. Then they **trample** it with their hard hooves.

hooves

**DID YOU KNOW?**
The name wildebeest came from the local people who call them "wild beasts".

# Who's hungry?

The crocodile is a **carnivore**. It eats other animals. The crocodile can go for almost a month without eating. Wildebeest are **herbivores**. They eat grasses.

**DID YOU KNOW?**
During the dry season the grass in the wildebeest's homeland dries up. So it joins two million other wildebeest looking for fresh grass.

# Danger below

The ground starts to shake! A **herd** of wildebeest has come to cross the river. But first they need a drink of water. The crocodile feels the **vibrations** of the stomping wildebeest. It gets ready for a fight.

A few wildebeest splash into the water. They walk out as far as they can. Then they start swimming towards the other side. Hundreds follow. The crocodile watches the wildebeest crossing the river.

The crocodile
looks for a young,
old, sick, or hurt
wildebeest to
attack.

17

The crocodile spots an old wildebeest. The wildebeest is not looking for **predators**. It is only focused on crossing the river. The crocodile whips its muscular tail from side to side to swim towards the old wildebeest.

**DID YOU KNOW?**
A crocodile will drag its **prey** underwater to drown it before eating it.

The crocodile quietly swims near the wildebeest **herd**. It sinks underwater. In a flash the crocodile chomps down on a wildebeest's leg. The wildebeest stabs at the crocodile with its horns. But its horns are no match for the crocodile's armour-like skin!

The crocodile is not letting go of the wildebeest's leg. It drags the wildebeest towards deeper water and pulls it under. It's trying to drown the wildebeest.

But the wildebeest bobs to the surface and grabs a breath. It struggles to swim. It's not giving up.

Other crocodiles swim to the scene. They work as a team. Now there is no way the wildebeest can escape. While the crocodiles are busy with the trapped wildebeest, the others quickly climb out of the river.

# And the winner is...

...the crocodile! The team of crocodiles rips off huge chunks of flesh. One adult wildebeest provides enough food for several crocodiles.

## DID YOU KNOW?

Crocodiles' jaws don't move sideways. So they cannot bite off chunks of meat. Instead they bite, then spin their bodies to rip off pieces of flesh.

# What are the odds?

Crocodiles catch their **prey** four out of every five tries! Crocodiles can eat up to half their body weight in food. Sometimes they catch and kill extra food. They store it underwater under a big rock until they are ready to eat it.

**DID YOU KNOW?**
About 200 people are eaten each year by Nile crocodiles.

# Glossary

**carnivore**  animal that eats meat

**herbivore**  animal that eats plants

**herd**  group of animals living and moving together

**hooves**  hard covering on animals' feet

**nostril**  nose opening

**predator**  animal that hunts other animals

**prey**  animal that is hunted by other animals for food

**trample**  walk heavily on something

**vibration**  shaking movement

# Find out more

## Books

*Alligators and Crocodiles,* Sally Morgan
(QED Publishing, 2007)

*Encyclopedia* of *Animals* (Dorling Kindersley,
2006)

*Serengeti Journey: On Safari in Africa,* Gare
Thompson (National Geographic Society, 2006)

## Websites

**http://animals.nationalgeographic.com/
animals/mammals/wildebeest.html**
This website is full of facts about wildebeest.

**http://kids.nationalgeographic.com/Animals/
CreatureFeature/Nile-crocodile**
Find out more about Nile crocodiles, watch a
video, and print off collector's cards.

# Index